Dominate Game Day
The Soccer Conditioning Blueprint You Need To Become an Elite Soccer Player

By Gregg Gillies, The Soccer Specialist
TheSoccerSpecialist.com

Published by Gregg Gillies

Disclaimer (AKA Legalese the Lawyers Require):

You must get your physician's approval before beginning this or any exercise program. These recommendations are not medical guidelines but are for educational purposes only. You must consult your physician prior to starting this program or if you have any medical condition or injury that contraindicates physical activity. This program is designed for healthy individuals 18 years and older only.

The information in this report is meant to supplement, not replace, proper exercise training. All forms of exercise pose some inherent risks. The editors and publishers advise readers to take full responsibility for their safety and know their limits. Before practicing the exercises in this book, be sure that your equipment is well-maintained, and do not take risks beyond your level of experience, aptitude, training, conditioning and fitness levels. The exercises and dietary programs in this book are not intended as a substitute for any exercise routine or treatment or dietary regimen that may have been prescribed by your physician.

Don't lift heavy weights if you are alone, inexperienced, injured, or fatigued. Don't perform any exercise unless you have been shown the proper technique by a certified personal trainer or certified strength and conditioning specialist. Always ask for instruction and assistance when lifting. Don't perform any exercise without proper instruction. Always do a warm-up prior to strength training and interval training.

See your physician before starting any exercise or nutrition program. If you are taking any medications, you must talk to your physician before starting any exercise program, including Advanced Arm Training. If you experience any lightheadedness, dizziness, or shortness of breath while exercising, stop the movement and consult a physician.

You must have a complete physical examination if you are sedentary, if you have high cholesterol, high blood pressure, or diabetes, if you are overweight, or if you are over 30 years old. Please discuss all nutritional changes with your physician or a registered dietician. If your physician recommends that you don't follow the program in this book, please follow your doctor's orders.

Foreword

First and foremost this book is dedicated to family. Without family, what are we?

As far as soccer goes, this book is dedicated to the Raptors. Thanks to them I've gotten to learn and grow as a coach and a person. I now have more patience than I thought it was a possible for a person to have!

I've gotten to watch these girls grow up and it's been exhausting, frustrating, annoying, nails on a chalkboard painful! It's also been a lot of fun and I'm proud of every single one of them, not just for their development as soccer players, but for their growth as people. Annoying, overly dramatic, pain in the butt, little people.

I would say a lot more nice things because some of them deserve it, but they might read this so I won't.

Raptors for Life

Ally Hovdestad

Ava Hutchinson

Ava Romero

Emily Broker

Grace Button

Isabella Kressel

Isabella Gigliotti

Jianna Lopez-Greer

Jillian Risell

Jocelyn Curillo

Jodie Lee

Julia Kellerman

Kaitlyn McDonald

Stephanie Pozega

Makayla Scott

Marisa Riley

Megan Turpin

Serenity Rivera

Shannon Murray

Shannon Smith

I'd say more about them individually but then I'll leave someone out and there will be lots of girl drama! Have you ever seen teen girl drama? It's not pretty!

About The Soccer Specialist

Gregg Gillies (aka The Soccer Specialist), is a Soccer Trainer, Head Coach and Youth Athlete Development Specialist who specializes in soccer players. Yeah, I know!

He has over twenty years of experience in the fitness conditioning and training world and holds multiple fitness and athlete development certifications, including as a youth development specialist, youth nutrition specialist and IYCA Endorsed Youth Kettlebell Instructor, with a focus on soccer players.

Coach Gregg is a passionate coach who loves inspiring athletes to commit to becoming the best player they can be while passing along a passion for the game as well as lessons that will serve them well in life off of the field, too.

The Soccer Specialist is also a nationally licensed soccer coach through the USSF.

He holds a variety of other licenses, diplomas and certifications in soccer and youth athlete development.

He has been a contributor to World Class Coaching, the premier educational resource for coaches (where the best go to learn from the best).

The Soccer Specialist specializes (imagine that!) in developing youth soccer players, where his focus is:

- maximizing and mastering a player's individual technical skills

- Improving their soccer IQ so they make better decisions on the field
- Focus on overall soccer specific athletic development, conditioning and fitness
- And most importantly, elevate their mental approach to the game, with the goal of helping them realize their soccer potential as well as preparing them for success in life after soccer.

He has also spoken at the Elite Youth Soccer Summit, put on by The Soccer Parent Life (ADD LINK), where the discussed the keys to developing young soccer players.

Coach Gregg also conducts personalized and customized online training programs for individual players that they can do at home to accelerate their development and take their game to the next level.

If you are interested in training with Coach Gregg go to http://thesoccerspecialist.com/contactcb

Introduction

This book is not long. There is not a lot of fluff. There are some tips and ideas in the introduction as to why the program is structured the way it is but 90% of the book is the actual program. You didn't get this book to read. You got it to get results. It's a book to be used!

There are diagrams and descriptions for the various drills for each session. However, seeing them can make them a lot easier to understand, so as a bonus for grabbing this book, I've created videos of each of the drills. If you grabbed this book early, it's possible the videos aren't ready yet but sign up below and you'll get emailed access as soon as they are completed.

I've also created a PDF with all the diagrams. For ebook readers, you might want a larger version and if you ordered the physical book, it's in black and white and the PDF will be in color.

To get videos of all the exercises in the conditioning program please go to the link below and put in your email address.

Access to the videos will be emailed to you for FREE! You'll also get a FREE Full Color PDF of the diagrams

==>> http://thesoccerspecialist.com/dominatebonus <<==

Run Soccer Player, Run!

Soccer players run. A lot. In fact, they run far more than other popular team sports. Now, before you run away screaming, let me tell you, the game of soccer is worth all that running! Just breathe, we're going to help you out with all that running.

This article charts the numbers in some typical sports <==

Here's the actual URL if you can't click that link (like if you're reading the hard copy version of this book) - https://www.businessinsider.com/chart-soccer-players-run-miles-2014-6

Baseball - .0375 miles (wow, that's just embarrassing, isn't it?)

American Football – 1.25 miles (for wide receivers and corner backs) – it's been determined by those that have a lot of time on their hands, that the average NFL game only contains about 11 minutes of live action in the three plus hours it takes to complete a game. That's a lot of rest. It's not an an easy sport, just a different type of 'conditioning.'

Basketball – 2.55 miles – It turns out basketball players don't do nearly the amount of running that most people thought. Growing up I typically heard numbers ranging from five to eight miles per game.

That being said, it's a lot of sprinting, lateral movement, explosiveness, agility and quickness. But they don't necessarily need a big endurance oriented aerobic base. And again, lots and lots of stoppages.

Especially if you get to the level where games are televised. There are 87 television timeouts and 17 team times outs per game (these numbers could very well be untrue and it just seems that way) so you have a lot of opportunity to catch your breath.

Tennis – 3 miles – this one can vary a lot depending on length of match, style of play and number of strokes. It's all short explosive movements, although if a point lasts a long time, it's can be a lot of short sprints with quick change of direction and that's not easy.

Field Hockey – 5.6 miles – Now we're getting somewhere. Good for them! But wait, the champ is here!

Soccer – 7 miles – It's a huge field (100 to 130 yards long and 50 to 80 yards wide) in a game that almost never stops, except for the players like Neymar who fall down and fake injuries all the time, bringing the game to a grinding halt.

And this is an average. Most midfielders run more. It's been said, according to SportVU (: https://gizmodo.com/5992583/how-far-do-you-run-in-different-sports) that some run as far as 9.5 miles.

This isn't a typical jogging pace. Soccer players have to utilize the same explosiveness, agility and quickness as basketball players. But they also have to do it while constantly changing speeds over a much greater variety of sprint distances. Combine that with the fact they have to do it while reacting to a lot more things that are happening at the same time so their brains are taxed more as well.

And do so with only one break in the action - halftime. Even when the ball goes out of bounds or a foul is committed the game doesn't stop. The team with possession can go right away.

A short sequence for a soccer player could involve an explosive sprint of five or ten yards, followed by a jump to head a ball, followed by a few seconds of walking, to a 20 yard sprint, a 10 yard jog, a 45 yard spring at 80% effort, to a 15 yard fast jog, followed by a full on 100% effort 80 yard sprint on the counterattack (or defending against one)!

Think of the long, intense runs of an outside back to overlap the midfielder out wide. That's tough enough. Now add in the fact of what that outside back must do if his team turns the ball over during or right after he's made that run!

What about the center back who goes all the way up the field and into the penalty box when her team has a corner kick that ends up being won by the other team who breaks out on a counterattack?

Or the typical demands of a box to box midfielder?

The forward that makes run after run behind the back line?

And that's not including the change of direction and all the other things a soccer player needs to worry about.

Here's a US 2014 World Cup game against Ghana. <==
https://www.businessinsider.com/chart-soccer-players-run-miles-2014-6

Michael Bradley ran the most, a distance of 7.9 miles.

He was followed by Kyle Beckerman (7.1 miles)

Jermaine Jones (7 miles)

Fabian Johnson (6.9 miles).

Only the center backs, goalie, substitutes (and players they went in for) ran less than 6.4 miles. Even the keeper, Tim Howard, covered 2.9 miles over the course of the game.

So it's true. Soccer players do have to run a lot. And at all different speeds, intensity, and distances. It takes real dedication and training to be able to be in the necessary condition to be a soccer player. And that's what we are going to do here.

While a soccer players needs a good baseline of endurance conditioning, ultimately soccer is an intensity sport. As players get older, there is less space and less time for players to make decisions and take action. They have to do so in a shorter period of time and do it with greater speed (and technical precision).

So soccer is about intensity and the speed of action. You'll hear coaches talk a lot about speed of play. This is what they mean. If your actions aren't taken quickly enough, they will not be successful. The higher the level, the more quickly those actions need to be taken, the more intense the game.

When it comes to conditioning, more is not necessarily better. Training smart, with intensity, is the key to building great conditioning so you are not so fatigued at the end of games that mistakes happen.

If speed of play is crucial to soccer success, you'll want to train smarter with a higher level of intensity. You can not play with a high level of speed if you are suffering from fatigue. If you don't recover from your training sessions, your training (including with the team) will suffer, eventually you'll hit the over training wall and you'll have a much higher risk of injury.

Of course you want to fatigue within your training session. But you don't want to still be fatigued for the next session. Your body needs to recover and repair before it can improve.

Your body needs to be able to perform more actions as the level of the game improves. This means you will have shorter recovery periods between actions. This is where interval training comes into play so that you can not only perform the necessary actions, but be able to recover more quickly between each action.

Let's give you a plan to get you match day fit so you can dominate at the end of games, while your opponents are wilting. Rule the last 15 minutes of a soccer match and rule the world! Or something like that. There might even be a ring involved.

We Are Not in Soccer Shape

There is a big difference between being "fit" or "in shape" and being in soccer shape. Here's a case in point. The girls team I've been coaching since they were 7 years old, entered high school recently. Every school the girls went to had some sort of conditioning test that was a variation of 'run 1.5 miles in under 12 minutes.'

At the school that had the specific 'run 1.5 miles in under 12 minutes' test, only a couple of girls actually made it and the rest had to run it again at another session. 14 and 15 year old club soccer players SHOULD have no problem passing that test.

But in this day and age of short attention spans and smart phones, most of them don't do anything outside of their team practices.

I've found that the players who are truly dedicated will put in the work if they are given a plan to follow and some support.

Why Being Fit Is So Important
And The Type Of Training You Need To Get
There

As you can see from above, you need a high degree of fitness for soccer so that you're able to be in the correct position on the pitch to be able to make a play.

However, it's not just about being able to do the necessary running. It's about being able to make the correct decisions and then execute technically. Making decisions, especially as quickly as you need to in a soccer match, is a lot tougher when you're physically exhausted.

In other words, you're a lot more likely to make a bad decision when you're tired. And that decision could cost your team the game.

Or you have a great chance to score, but because you're exhausted, your technique suffers, and what should be a simple tap in gets pushed wide because you didn't get your feet set correctly.

When you're fit, everything else about your game will be better.

Game Plan

While typical slow go cardio, such as running 10 miles at a slow pace, isn't going to do a whole lot for your soccer conditioning, you do need to develop some type of aerobic base.

So this means combining aerobic, or steady state cardio with interval training sessions to develop the necessary conditioning to excel in a soccer match.

Numerous studies have shown that high intensity interval training workouts increase both one's aerobic and anaerobic workout capacity while endurance training just improves the former.

It has also been shown that intense interval training actually increases aerobic capacity to a better degree than traditional low intensity aerobics.

G. Rhodas, et al, "A Short Training Programme for the Rapid Improvement of Both Aerobic and Anaerobic Metabolism," *European Journal of Applied Physiology* *82.5-6 (2000):480-486*

Interval training is intense, and while you will improve your aerobic and endurance capacity, you also highly tax your anerobic system as well.

It's much more like a weight training workout, as far as how it affects your muscles. This means you shouldn't do high intensity interval training workouts more than 3 or 4 times per week, and these workouts should NOT be long!

Interval training focuses on quality over quantity.

The most famous study done on interval training, by Dr. Tabata on world class speed skaters, involved all out work for 20 seconds, followed by 10 seconds of rest, repeated 8 times. **Yes, that's a FOUR MINUTE WORKOUT!**

And the speed skaters all significantly improved their aerobic and anerobic capacity.

Numerous studies have shown that this type of interval training increases both one's aerobic and anaerobic workout capacity while endurance training just improves the former. In addition, it has been shown that interval training actually increases aerobic capacity to a better degree than traditional low intensity aerobics.

G. Rhodas, et al, "A Short Training Programme for the Rapid Improvement of Both Aerobic and Anaerobic Metabolism," *European Journal of Applied Physiology* 82.5-6 (2000):480-486

A. Tremblay, et al, "Impact on Exercise Intensity on Body Fatness and Skeletal Muscle Metabolism," *Metabolism* 43.7 (1994):814-818

I. Tabata, et al, "Metabolic Profile of High Intensity Intermittent Exercises," *Med. Sci. Sports Exerc.* 29.3 (1997): 390-395

I. Tabata, et al, "Effects of Moderate Intensity Endurance and High Intensity Intermittent Training on Anaerobic Capacity and VO2max," *Med. Sci. Sports Exerc.* 28.10 (1996):1327-1330

The above Tabata study also showed a 14 percent increase in aerobic fitness and a 28 percent increase in anaerobic capacity in only 14 weeks when following a high intensity training program.

Of course, what non one talks about with regard to that study, is the incredible level of intensity reached by those speed skaters, a threshold very, very few people could match.

It doesn't mean interval training isn't important, it most certainly is. It just means the dream of a four minute work that transforms your body and gives you the conditioning level of an Olympic athlete or elite level professional soccer player is probably out of reach for now.

"Interval training stresses energy systems in the body that aren't accustomed to being used," says Jeramie Hinojosa, M.S., director of the East Texas Medical Center Olympic Center, in Tyler, Texas. "Blood supply to cells increases, the cells use oxygen more efficiently, and the enzymes that help create energy also increase. This improves fitness."

Keep in mind, serious sprint workouts are similar to intense weight training sessions for the legs, so your body needs time to recover. If you start doing multiple sprinting sessions per week, while also weight training, cut back on your leg workouts with weights accordingly.

There are numerous ways to perform not only sprinting sessions, but interval training in general, from work to rest ratio, length of work and rest intervals, number of interval 'set's, exercises involved, etc

Don't Neglect Technical Skills

This is soccer and ball skills are very important, right? So we'll be combining ball work into the conditioning sessions so you'll not only improve your fitness but your ball control and dribbling as well.

The conditioning program will consist of four training days per week. Remember, the focus is solely on improving conditioning and fitness levels. There is no strength training or speed, agility (SAQ) and quickness training, either. Although, you'll get some of that inadvertently, but no mini hurdles or agility ladders will be in use.

You can perform dedicated skills work on other days. That being said, two days a week will involve a lot of touches on the ball.

You can break up the training sessions however you like, but I would not train more than two days in a row. A typical set up I would recommend would look like the following:

Training Session #1 – Monday
Training Session #2 – Tuesday
Training Session #3 – Thursday
Training Session # 4 – Friday

You could do Tuesday, Wednesday, Friday and Saturday if that works best for your schedule. The most important thing is the consistency of the schedule. The more days you skip, the less effective the conditioning program is going to be for you.

Progressive Overload Training

Progressive overload training is a weight training concept. In weight training, it's the idea of increasing the number of repetitions you can perform with a weight until you hit a certain number like 12. Then at the next workout you increase the weight. Over time, you become stronger.

We will be incorporating this idea into the conditioning program. As your body adapts, you'll be able to do more work at a higher intensity.

Train Hard

The program works. You will get more fit, better conditioned and be able to play longer and harder. However, if you do nothing, that's exactly what you'll get out of the program, nothing.

If you give it 80% you'll get some decent results.

The point is, if you make your workouts and put in 100% effort, you will see great results.

Important Note: Making Adjustments To The Program

This program assumes you are in some type of condition for soccer. If you haven't been playing or training for awhile, are coming off a long layoff, maybe you've been injured, this program is not for you.

However, you can modify it by shortening the workouts and / or lessening the intensity. Or consider starting with a couple of weeks of steady state cardio before jumping in to this type of program.

Go here and contact me - http://thesoccerspecialist.com/contactcb

For Pre-Teens

If you are a pre-teen, start with less than all out intensity AND cut the volume in half. If it asks for 6 sets of something, only perform 3 sets.

If it's a 2 mile run, go for a 1 mile run.

Again, contact me here - http://thesoccerspecialist.com/contactcb

Adjusting To Fit In With Off- Season Training

You might still be practicing with your team, or training with someone individually, or even playing another sport. In that case, you'll want to make some adjustments to the program.

For example, if you are training with your team twice a week for 90 minutes in the off-season, you can reduce the conditioning training down to twice per week, or even once, depending on how active you are at the time.

Which sessions you do will be influenced by your other training. If your team does a lot of running within its soccer training or does separate conditioning, sessions you might consider only doing the two sessions with the ball and reducing the length of some of the drills.

Dribbling

For the sessions that include ball work, it's important to focus on taking a dribble with every step. As you get more comfortable with this style you'll be able to dribble faster and faster. This is key, not just for game performance but also to get the most out of the conditioning drills that include a ball

Except when you are cutting and changing direction, you should be focused on toe down and dribbling with the laces and getting a touch on the ball with every step. The greatest in the world at this is Lionel Messi.

If there is one skill that can elevate your game to the next level it's the ability to dribble with every step you take. You'll always have the ball at your feet and be able to change direction from any oncoming defender.

Yes, this is a conditioning program but by focusing on this dribbling technique you can completely change your game.

If you're not sure, contact me with questions: http://thesoccerspecialist.com/contactcb

To get videos of the exercises in the conditioning program please go to the link below and put in your email address.

Access to the videos will be emailed to you for FREE! You'll also get a FREE Full Color PDF of the diagrams

==>> http://thesoccerspecialist.com/dominatebonus <<==

Training Tip: Some of the sessions are ball skill patterns such as Bells, or lateral patterns such as inside left foot to outside right foot and reverse. In order to get the most out of the conditioning and intensity of these drills, you may want to familiarize yourself with the patterns before doing the workout.

This way you can perform them at a high intensity instead of spending most of the training time learning the pattern, which means doing it more slowly.

It's time for YOU to reach YOUR goals!

Remember Vince Lombardi!

> "We will be relentless in our pursuit for perfection.
> We won't ever be perfect – but in the process we will achieve greatness."

Big Goals, Big Results!

Here we go!

Dominate Game Day
4 Week Soccer Fitness Program

Warm ups

Always perform a five to ten minute warm up before each session. If you have a warm up you already use that works for you (maybe something you use before team sessions), that's fine. There are many effective warms ups. All of them should use some form of dynamic work to get the body warmed up and ready to move.

Here's an example of a warm up you can use before each session.

Single Leg Step and Reach
Lunge + Hamstring Stretch
Walking Toe Grabs
Walking Knee Grabs
Toy Soldiers
Easy Knee Up Skips
Feet to Butt Jog
Single Leg Hops
Side Shuffles
Leg Rotation In to Out Shuffle
Leg Rotation Out to In Shuffle
Front to Back Leg Swings x 15 per leg
Side-to-Side Leg Swings x 15 per leg
Short Sprints progressing the intensity

All of these are done for a distance of 10 – 15 yards, except the sprints which can run from 10 to 40 yards. How many sprints is individual. Probably a few more at the higher distances on sprint days.

Before any of the sessions with a ball, spend a couple of minutes of dribbling and add the ball to the short sprint build up.

It's important to spend some time cooling down after an intense session. Now is the time to hit a few more traditional static stretches.

Cool Down

1 Kneeling Hip Flexor w/ Reach
2 Kneeling Front Hamstring
3 Kneeling Quadricep
4 Stretch Lunge

If you have a foam roller, and are feeling extra tight, consider some simple foam rolling work each day as well, or at least after your training sessions.

Some examples include:

1 Calf Rolls
2 Shin Rolls
3 IT Band
4 Hip Flexors
5 Glutes
6 Hamstrings
7 Lower Back

Adjust your warm up and cool down as you see fit. Questions? Go here – http://thesoccerspecialist.com/contactcb

Dominate Game Day Week 1

Day 1 – Workout 1

Exercise	Sets	Time	Rest
Warm up	1	5 – 10 minutes	1 – 2 minutes
2 mile run	1	For time	NA

Day 2 – Workout 2 - With The Ball

Exercise	Sets	Time	Rest
Warm Up	1	5 – 10 minutes	1 – 2 minutes
Bells	2	30 seconds	30 seconds
3 Bells to Outside Touch	2	30 seconds	30 seconds
Bell Bell Outside Rip Back	2	30 seconds	30 seconds
Outside Outside Stop	2	30 seconds	30 seconds
Outside Touch Scissor	2	30 seconds	30 seconds
Freestyle Dribble (2 yds x 2 yds)	5	45 seconds	30 seconds
10 Yard Turn Dribble	10	NA	20 seconds
Small T Dribble	8 sets (4 per foot)	NA	45 seconds

Descriptions

Bells, also known as Side to Sides or Foundations are simply tapping the ball with the inside of one foot to the inside of the other foot and back. You stay in place as if the ball is on an imaginary line from one foot to the other. The ball stays between the legs on the ground.

Here are a few foot skill videos:

Bell Bell Outside Rip Back -
https://raptorsfootskills.s3.amazonaws.com/bellbelloutsideripback.mp4
Outside Outside Stop
https://raptorsfootskills.s3.amazonaws.com/outsideoutsidestop.mp4
Outside Touch Scissor
https://raptorsfootskills.s3.amazonaws.com/outsidetouchscissor.mp4

** Be sure and grab all the foot skill videos above, and all the other drills on video as well.

Every drill and foot skill pattern on video ==>>
http://thesoccerspecialist.com/dominatebonus

Freestyle Dribble

In a 2 yard by 2 yard square (use cones, socks or whatever to mark the area). At a high intensity get as many touches and make as many moves as possible. Be creative do whatever you like, use your imagination. Use all parts of your foot, inside, outside, heel, sole.

Perform 5 sets of 45 seconds each with a rest of 30 seconds between sets.

10 Yard Sprint Turn

Set up cones 10 yards apart. Starting at one cone, speed dribble to the other cone (touch the ball with every step), cut and dribble back to the start. That's one set. Alternate feet. For example, on the first set, only use the right foot. On the second set, only use the left foot and so on. Perform 10 sets with 20 seconds of rest between sets.

Dribble as quickly as possible from the start around the far cone and back. Stop the ball directly next to the starting cone before resting and performing the next set.

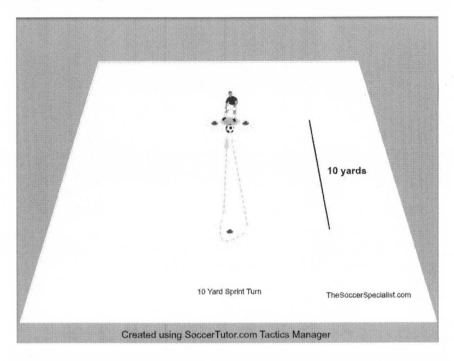

10 yards

10 Yard Sprint Turn

TheSoccerSpecialist.com

Created using SoccerTutor.com Tactics Manager

Small T Dribble

Perform 4 sets with each foot for 8 total sets. Rest 45 seconds between each set.

For each set, alternate the way you turn at the first cone. For example, if you start to the right on one set, then start to the left on the next set.

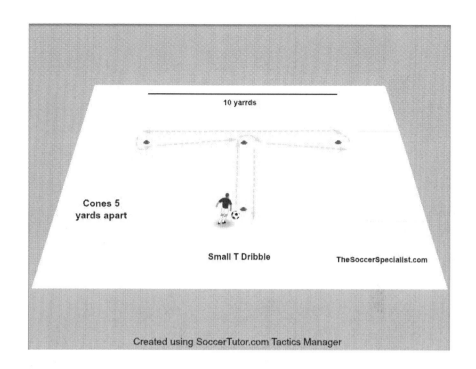

Small T Dribble

TheSoccerSpecialist.com

Created using SoccerTutor.com Tactics Manager

Day 3 - Rest

Day 4 - Without The Ball

Exercise	Sets	Time	Rest (Walk)
Warm Up	1	5 – 10 minutes	1 – 2 minutes
Run	2	1 minute	3 minutes
Run	2	45 seconds	2 minutes
Run	3	30 seconds	90 seconds
Run	4	20 seconds	90 seconds
Run	5	10 seconds	60 seconds

If that's confusing to follow it goes like this. You simply alternate the shorter run time with the rest (or walk) time.

Interval Workout

1 minute run – 3 minute walk x 2 sets
45 second run – 2 minute walk x 2 sets
30 second run – 1 ½ minute walk x 3 sets
20 second run – 1 ½ minute walk x 4 sets
10 second run – 1 minute walk x 5 sets

Day 5 – Workout With the Ball

Exercise	Sets	Time	Rest (Walk)
Warm Up	1	5 – 10 minutes	1 – 2 minutes
Pro Agility Drill With the Ball	10 (5 per foot)	NA	45 seconds
Star Dribbling	8 (4 per foot)	NA	1 minute
40/40 Speed Dribble	4 (2 per foot)	NA	2 minutes
Shuttle Run (5-10-5-10)	4 (2 per foot)	NA	1 minute

Pro Agility Drill with Ball

Remember, a dribble with every step. Alternate feet each round.

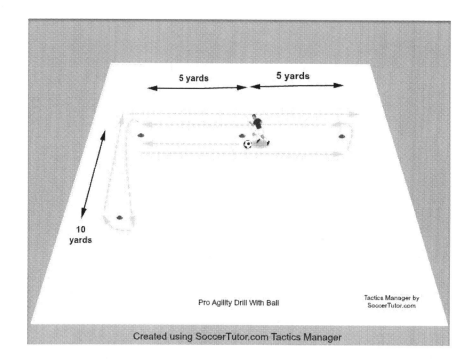

5 yards   5 yards

10 yards

Pro Agility Drill With Ball

Tactics Manager by
SoccerTutor.com

Created using SoccerTutor.com Tactics Manager

Star Dribbling

Perform a sharp change of direction cut at each cone, either inside or outside of dribbling foot (or Cruyff). Don't pull the ball back, make a sharp 180 degree cut instead.

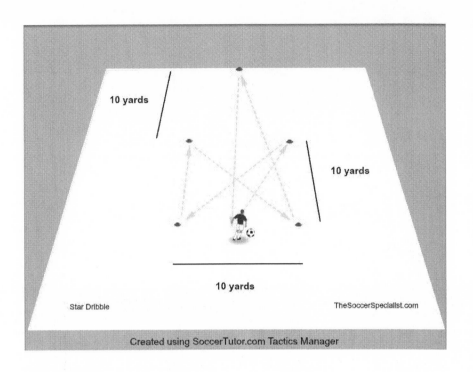

40 yard / 40 yard speed dribble

40 yards up and back = 80 yards per set – 1 set per foot. 2 minutes of rest. Every step is a dribble.

Shuttle Run (5-10-5-10)

One complete round is 5 yards and back, then 10 yards and back, then 5 yards and back and then 10 yards and back. That's one round. Perform 4 rounds, 2 with each foot.

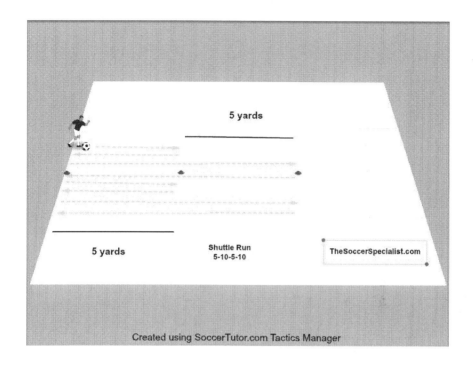

Day 6 – Rest

Day 7 – Rest

To get videos of the exercises in the conditioning program please go to the link below and put in your email address.

Access to the videos will be emailed to you for FREE! You'll also get a FREE Full Color PDF of the diagrams

==>> http://thesoccerspecialist.com/dominatebonus <<==

Dominate Game Day Week 2

Day 1 – Workout 1

Exercise	Sets	Time	Rest
Warm up	1	5 – 10 minutes	1 – 2 minutes
1 mile run	2	For time	2 minutes

Run 1 mile.
Rest 2 minutes.
Run 1 mile.

Day 2 – Workout 2 - With the Ball

Exercise	Sets	Time	Rest
Warm Up	1	5-10 minutes	1 – 2 minutes
Toe Taps	2	30 seconds	30 seconds
Bells	2	30 seconds	30 seconds
Bell Bell Outside Rip Back	2	30 seconds	30 seconds
Sole Rolls (Side to Side)	2	30 seconds	30 seconds
Inside Right to Outside Left to Inside Left to Outside Right (Repeat)	2	30 seconds	30 seconds
Toe Taps	2	30 seconds	30 seconds
Inside Left to Outside Left	2	30 seconds	30 seconds

Inside Right to Outside Right	2	30 seconds	30 seconds
Push Pull Left	2	30 seconds	30 seconds
Push Pull Right	2	30 seconds	30 seconds

Be sure and get all the videos for FREE!

==>> http://thesoccerspecialist.com/dominatebonus <<==

Day 3 – Rest

Day 4 – Workout 3 - Without The Ball

Exercise	Sets	Time	Rest
Warm up	1	5 – 10 minutes	1 – 2 minutes
100 yard sprint	6	NA	2 minutes
50 yard sprint	6	NA	90 seconds
Squat Thrusts	5	30 seconds	30 seconds

Warm up: Very important here. Focus on the sprint build up portion of the warm up. If it takes an extra sprint of two at 75% to 85% effort, make it happen.

Sprints are self-explanatory.

The squat thrust is simply a body weight squat. At the bottom lean forwards and put your hands on the ground then kick your legs out behind you until they are straight and you are on your toes. This puts your body in a plank or top of a push up position. Then bring your legs back in and stand back up.

Day 5 – Workout 4 – With The Ball

Exercise	Sets	Time	Rest
Warm up	1	5 – 10 minutes	1 – 2 minutes
Big T Heart Drill x 3	2	NA	4 minutes
Shuttle Run (5-10)	8 (4 per foot)	NA	35 seconds
Split V Dribble	6 (3 per foot)	NA	25 seconds

Big T Heart Drill x 3

Follow the yellow lines first (see image below). When you get back to the start, follow the red line, which starts the same pattern on the other side. Once back to the start, that's one complete round.

You will do 3 complete rounds non-stop then rest four minutes and repeat one more time. Alternate feet each round, so you'll be doing three rounds per foot.

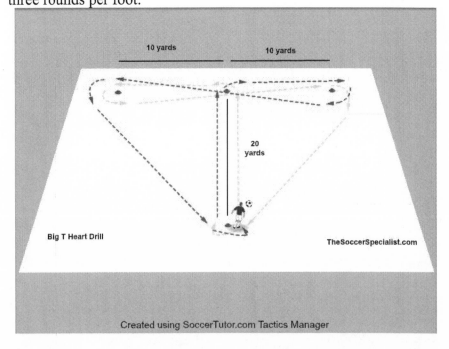

Shuttle Run (5-10)

Place 3 cones in a line 5 yards apart. Dribble out with one foot to the second cone and back and then dribble out to the third cone and back. Alternate feet.

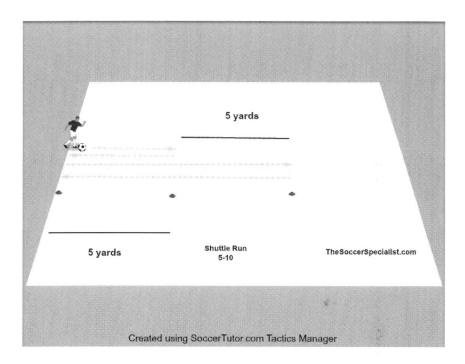

Split V Dribble (see diagram below)

Start to the left first (the yellow line), then go to the right (the red line) then straight up the middle.

Remember, one dribble with every step.

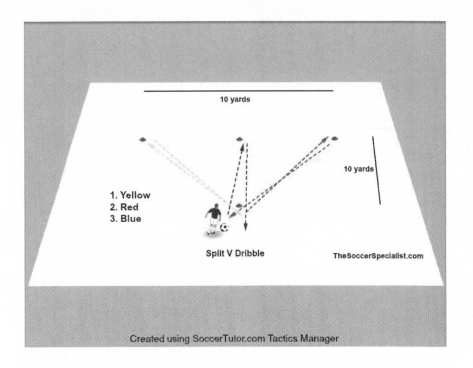

Day 6 – Rest

Day 7 – Rest

To get videos of the exercises in the conditioning program please go to the link below and put in your email address.

Access to the videos will be emailed to you for FREE! You'll also get a FREE Full Color PDF of the diagrams

==>> http://thesoccerspecialist.com/dominatebonus <<==

Dominate Game Day Week 3

Day 1 – Workout 1

Exercise	Sets	Time	Rest
Warm up	1	5 – 10 minutes	1 – 2 minutes
3 mile run	1	For time	NA

Day 2 – Workout 2 - With the Ball

Exercise	Sets	Time	Rest
Warm Up	1	5-10 minutes	1 – 2 minutes
Figure 8 Speed Dribble	6 (3 per foot)	45 seconds	30 seconds
Line Speed Dribble	6 (3 per foot)	45 seconds	30 seconds
Pro Agility Drill With The Ball	8 (4 per foot)	NA	30 seconds
Bells	8	30 seconds	30 seconds

Figure 8 Speed Dribble

See diagram below. Place cones 10 yards apart. For each round use the same foot the entire time. This will allow for the inside of the foot on one turn and the outside of the foot on the other turn. Switch feet for each round. Remember, try and get one dribble on every step.

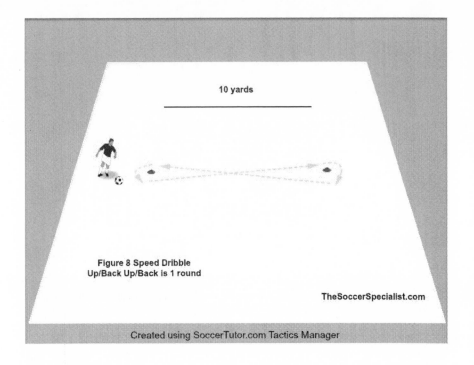

10 yards

Figure 8 Speed Dribble
Up/Back Up/Back is 1 round

Line Speed Dribble

Like the figure 8 speed dribble drill the end cones are 10 yards apart. Add a second cone at each end about a yard or so from the cone already there. This gives you a lane to work in so that you can make sure you are dribbling straight and cutting sharply.

Instead of going around the end cone like with the figure 8 you make a sharp 180 degree cut at each end. Do not use the sole of the foot to pull it back. Use a nice chop cut with the inside of the foot (this can be a normal cut or a Cruyff).

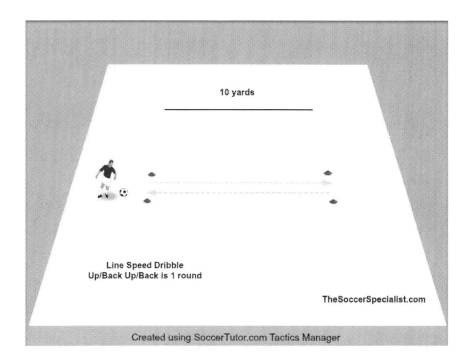

Pro Agility Drill With The Ball

Remember, a dribble with every step. Alternate feet each round.

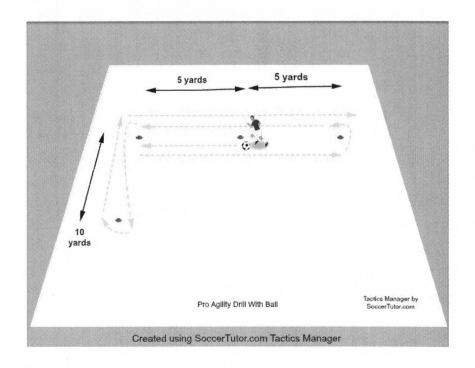

Pro Agility Drill With Ball

Tactics Manager by
SoccerTutor.com

Created using SoccerTutor.com Tactics Manager

Bells

Also known as side to sides or foundations, bells are simply quick
side to side touches with the inside of each foot, back and forth. See
video here (insert)

Day 3 – Rest

Day 4 - Without The Ball

Exercise	Sets	Time	Rest (Walk)
Warm Up	1	5 – 10 minutes	1 – 2 minutes
Speed Mountain Climbers	8	20 seconds	10 seconds (2 minutes rest after last set before next exercise)
Pro Agility	5	NA	1 minute

Drill (no ball) x 2			
Run *	3	30 seconds	90 seconds
Run *	4	20 seconds	90 seconds
Run *	5	10 seconds	60 seconds

* For the interval runs if you are in an area where it is easier to mark off a distance than run for time for this session, you can substitute 200 yards, 100 yards, and 50 yards for the times of 30, 20 and 10 seconds respectively.

Speed Mountain Climbers

Perform these quickly, without letting the feet touch the ground when you pull the knee up to your chest.

Pro Agility Drill Without the Ball x 2

Complete the drill two times before resting. Each set is the drill being completed twice without rest.

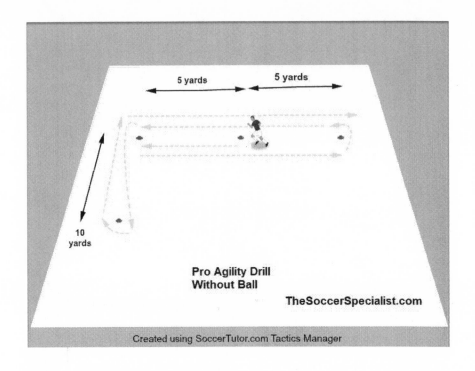

Pro Agility Drill Without Ball

TheSoccerSpecialist.com

Created using SoccerTutor.com Tactics Manager

Day 5 – Workout With The Ball

Exercise	Sets	Time	Rest (Walk)
Warm Up	1	5 – 10 minutes	1 – 2 minutes
Soccer Gasser (with ball)	1 (alternate feet on the up and back)	NA	3 minutes
Shuttle Dribble (10-20)	8 (4 per foot)	NA	45 seconds
30 Yard Sprint	10 (5 per foot)	NA	30 seconds
3 Move Sequence (Step Over/Outside Touch, Cruyff, L Behind)	5	45 seconds	30 seconds

Soccer Gasser With The Ball

Old time athletes would call these suicides. They are popular in basketball as well. If you don't have a lined field, you can mark off cones at 18, 50, 82 and 100 yards.

You dribble out 18 yards (top of the penalty area) and back to the start.

Then out 50 yards (or midfield) and back to the start.

Dribble out 82 yards (to the top of the other 18 or penalty box) and back to the start.

Dribble from the start to the other end line and back. That's one round.

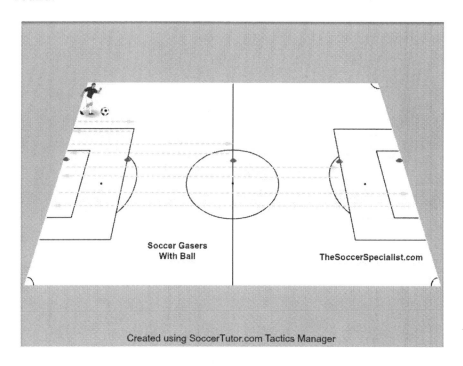

Soccer Gasers
With Ball

TheSoccerSpecialist.com

Created using SoccerTutor.com Tactics Manager

Shuttle Dribble (10-20)

Place three cones at the start, 10 yards out and 20 yards out. Dribble out 10 yards and back then dribble out 20 yards and back. That's one round.

30 Yard Sprint

Speed dribble (a dribble for every step) 30 yards. Rest 30 seconds. Then dribble 30 yards back. Every 30 yards is one round. So up, rest and back is two rounds.

3 Move Sequence (Step Over/Outside Touch, Cruyff, L Behind)

Dribble around freestyle and try and complete as many of the 3 Move Sequence as possible.

To get videos of the exercises in the conditioning program please go to the link below and put in your email address.

Access to the videos will be emailed to you for FREE! You'll also get a FREE Full Color PDF of the diagrams

==>> http://thesoccerspecialist.com/dominatebonus <<==

Day 6 – Rest

Day 7 – Rest

Dominate Game Day Week 4

Day 1 – Workout 1

Exercise	Sets	Time	Rest
Warm up	1	5 – 10 minutes	1 – 2 minutes
1 mile run	3	For time	2 minutes (rest/walk)

Day 2 – Workout 2 - With the Ball

Exercise	Sets	Time	Rest
Warm Up	1	5-10 minutes	1 – 2 minutes
Toe Taps	2	40 seconds	20 seconds
Bells	2	40 seconds	20 seconds
Bell Bell Outside Rip Back	2	40 seconds	20 seconds
Sole Rolls (Side to Side)	2	40 seconds	20 seconds
Inside Right to Outside Left to Inside Left to Outside Right (Repeat)	2	40 seconds	20 seconds
Toe Taps	2	40 seconds	20 seconds
Inside Left to Outside Left	2	40 seconds	20 seconds
Inside Right to	2	40 seconds	20 seconds

Outside Right			
Push Pull Left	2	40 seconds	20 seconds
Push Pull Right	2	40 seconds	20 seconds
Shuttle Run (5-10)	10 (5 per foot)	NA	45 seconds)

Day 3 – Rest

Day 4 - Without The Ball

Exercise	Sets	Time	Rest (Walk)
Warm Up	1	5 – 10 minutes	1 – 2 minutes
400 Yard Sprint	4	NA	2 minutes
200 Yard Sprint	3	NA	90 seconds
100 Yard Sprint	2	NA	45 seconds

If you have access to a track, you can substitute 1 lap for 400 yards, a half lap for 200 yards and a quarter lap for 100 yards.

If you are at a field but don't have that much room, you can set up 100 yards (or use a soccer field) and go up/back, up/back for 400 yards, up/back for 200 yards and the length of the field for 100 yards.

Day 5 – Workout With The Ball

Exercise	Sets	Time	Rest (Walk)
Warm Up	1	5 – 10 minutes	1 – 2 minutes
Cone Weave	8 (4 per foot)	NA	20 seconds

Line Speed Dribble x 2	6 (3 per foot)	NA	45 seconds
Star Dribbling	3	NA	90 seconds
50/50 Speed Dribble	2	NA	2 minutes

Cone Weave

Set cones up as shown in the diagram below.

The cones that are in a straight line (every other cone in the diagram) are 10 yards apart. So from start to finish it's 30 yards. Dribble to the outside of each cone. Stop at the far end. Rest and then repeat for the noted number of rounds.

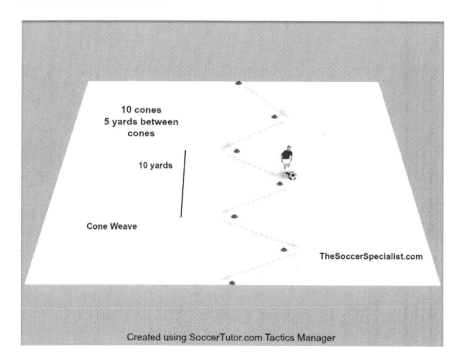

Line Speed Dribbling x 2

For this drill, you will dribble up and back twice to equal one set.

Focus on dribbling with every stride and make a sharp cut at the cone. Don't turn around the cone or pull the ball back.

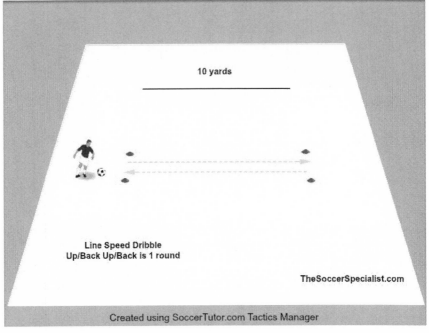

Star Dribbling

Perform a sharp change of direction cut at each cone, either inside or outside of dribbling foot (or Cruyff). Don't pull the ball back, make a sharp 180 degree cut instead.

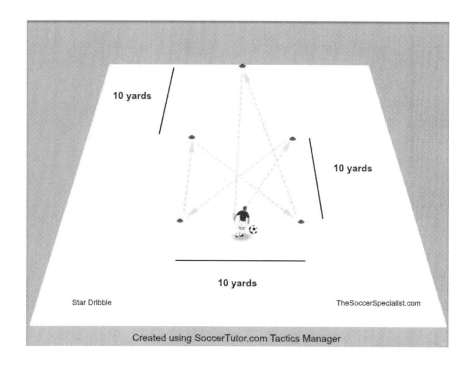

50/50 Speed Dribbling

Simply dribble out 50 yards (dribble on every step) and back 50 yards. That's one set.

Day 6 – Rest

Day 7 – Rest

Congratulations! You are finished!!! I feel bad for the teams you are going to play! They'll be sucking wind, hands on hips while you're racing around the field making plays, as if you are twice as quick, fast, smart and skilled as they are! Well done!

If you read through the program to see what it's about and haven't gotten your free videos, do so now!

To get videos of the exercises in the conditioning program please go to the link below and put in your email address.

Access to the videos will be emailed to you for FREE! You'll also get a FREE Full Color PDF of the diagrams

==>> http://thesoccerspecialist.com/dominatebonus <<==

If you have any questions, please don't hesitate to contact me – http://thesoccerspecialist.com/contactcb

If you enjoyed this program, it would mean a lot if you could go to Amazon and leave a 5 star review. The more great reviews I get, the more notice the book gets, the more sales I make. And that leaves me with more time creating content and programs that can help youth soccer players get to the next level of their development. Thanks!

Good luck!

Remember Vince Lombardi!

> "We will be relentless in our pursuit for perfection.
> We won't ever be perfect – but in the process we will
> achieve greatness."

Big Goals, Big Results!

Coach Gregg, The Soccer Specialist ==>
http://thesoccerspecialist.com

Made in the USA
Las Vegas, NV
29 December 2021

39739509R00030